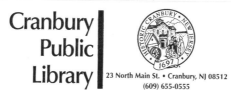

What Can Build?

Patricia Whitehouse

Heinemann Library
Chicago, Illinois

Customer Service 888-454-2279
Visit our website at www.heinemannlibrary.com

Designed by Sue Emerson, Heinemann Library; Page layout by Que-Net Media™
Printed and bound in the U.S.A. by Lake Book Manufacturing
Photo research by Bill Broyles

08 07 06 05 04
10 9 8 7 6 5 4 3 2 1

Library of Congress Cataloging-in-Publication Data
Whitehouse, Patricia, 1958-
 What can build? / Patricia Whitehouse.
   v. cm. – (What can?)
Contents: What is building? – How do living things build? – Can bugs build? – Can spiders build? – Can birds build? – Can furry animals build? – Can animals build underwater? – Can machines build? – Can people build?
 ISBN 1-4034-4370-X (HC), 1-4034-4377-7 (Pbk.)
 1. Nest building–Juvenile literature. 2. Animals–Habitations–Juvenile literature. 3. Building–Juvenile literature.
[1. Nest building. 2. Animals–Habitations. 3. Building.] I. Title.
 QL756.W46 2003
 591.56'4–dc21

2003001015

Acknowledgments
The author and publishers are grateful to the following for permission to reproduce copyright material:
p. 4 Fritz Polking/Frank Lane Picture Agency/Corbis; p. 5 PhotoDisc; p. 6 Steve Solum/Bruce Coleman Inc.; p. 7L Alan & Sandy Carey/Oxford Scientific Films; pp. 7R, 11 Oxford Scientific Films; pp. 8, 17 Dwight Kuhn/DRK Photo; p. 9L C. P. Hickman/Visuals Unlimited; p. 9R Philip Richardson/Gallo Images/Corbis; p. 10 Jane McAlonan/Visuals Unlimited; p. 12 Gerard Fuehrer/Visuals Unlimited; p. 13 Roger Tory Peterson/DRK Photo; p. 14 Wayne Lankinen/DRK Photo; p. 15 Gerald & Buff Corsi/Visuals Unlimited; p. 16L David B. Fleetham/Visuals Unlimited; p. 16R Norbert Wu/DRK Photo; p. 18 Charles O'Rear/Corbis; p. 19 Galen Rowell/Corbis; p. 20 Robert Lifson/Heinemann Library; p. 21 Audrey Gibson/Visuals Unlimited; p. 22 (row 1, L-R) Jane McAlonan/Visuals Unlimited, Gerard Fuehrer/Visuals Unlimited, Wayne Lankinen/DRK Photo; (row 2, L-R) Charles O'Rear/Corbis, Audrey Gibson/Visuals Unlimited; p. 23 (row 1, L-R) Roger Tory Peterson/DRK Photo, Gerald & Buff Corsi/Visuals Unlimited, Charles O'Rear/Corbis, C. P. Hickman/Visuals Unlimited; (row 2, L-R) John Luke/Index Stock Imagery, Jane McAlonan/Visuals Unlimited, Oxford Scientific Films; (row 3, L-R) David B. Fleetham/Visuals Unlimited, Gerard Fuehrer/Visuals Unlimited, Dwight Kuhn/DRK Photo, Corbis; (row 4) Frank Staub/Index Stock Imagery; p. 24 (row 1, L-R) Jane McAlonan/Visuals Unlimited, Audrey Gibson/Visuals Unlimited; (row 2, L-R) Gerard Fuehrer/Visuals Unlimited, Wayne Lankinen/DRK Photo; (row 3) Charles O'Rear/Corbis; back cover (L-R) Dwight Kuhn/DRK Photo, Gerald & Buff Corsi/Visuals Unlimited

Cover photograph by Niall Benvie/Corbis

Every effort has been made to contact copyright holders of any material reproduced in this book.
Any omissions will be rectified in subsequent printings if notice is given to the publisher.

Special thanks to our advisory panel for their help in the preparation of this book:

Alice Bethke, Library Consultant
Palo Alto, CA

Eileen Day, Preschool Teacher
Chicago, IL

Kathleen Gilbert,
Second Grade Teacher
Round Rock, TX

Sandra Gilbert,
Library Media Specialist
Fiest Elementary School
Houston, TX

Jan Gobeille,
Kindergarten Teacher
Garfield Elementary
Oakland, CA

Angela Leeper,
Educational Consultant
Wake Forest, NC

Some words are shown in bold, **like this.**
You can find them in the picture glossary on page 23.

Contents

What Is Building?

Things that build make something.

Builders make things with **materials**.

People and some animals build with tools.

Other living things build with parts of their bodies.

How Do Living Things Build?

First, builders need to find **materials** to build with.

Then, they carry the materials where they are going to build.

Some builders stick materials together.

Some builders just put materials in place.

Can Bugs Build?

Wasps are bugs that build.

Paper wasps mix spit with **wood** to build their **nests.**

termites

tower

Termites are bugs that build towers.

Some termite towers are taller than your house.

Can Spiders Build?

Garden spiders build webs with **silk**.

They use the webs to catch food.

Trap-door spiders build a door over a hole in the ground.

They hide under the door to catch bugs.

Can Birds Build?

Many birds build **nests**.

Orioles build nests that look like bags.

Guira cuckoos do not build nests.

They lay their eggs in nests built by other birds.

Can Furry Animals Build?

Beavers are furry animals that live near rivers and ponds.

They use sticks to build **dams** and homes.

Gorillas are big and furry.

They build **nests** out of grass.

Can Animals Build Underwater?

Tiny coral animals build a wall.

Millions of tiny walls make
a **coral reef**.

nest

Father **stickleback fish** build **nests.**

Mother sticklebacks lay eggs in the nests.

Can Machines Build?

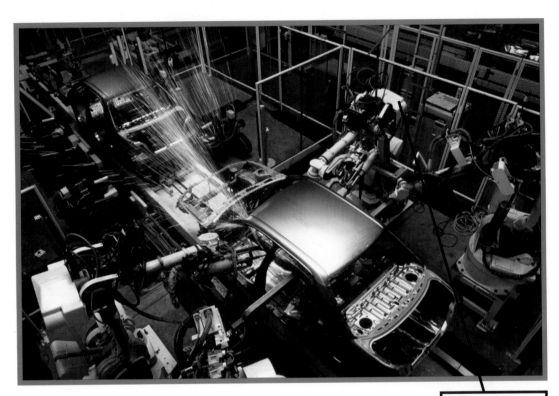

robot

Robots are machines that can help build cars.

But people have to make the robots work.

18

Machines help people build.

A worker is using a crane to lift **materials.**

Can People Build?

People build lots of things.

Children can build a hideout.

People can build houses.

This person is building a wall
of bricks.

Quiz

Which of these things can build?

Can you find them in the book?

Picture Glossary

beaver
page 14

materials
pages 4, 6,
7, 19

robot
page 18

termites
page 9

coral reef
page 16

nest
pages 8, 12,
13, 15, 17

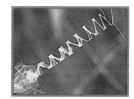

silk
page 10

**trap-door
spider**
page 11

dam
page 14

oriole
(OH-ree-ohl)
page 12

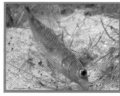

**stickleback
fish**
page 17

wood
page 8

Guira cuckoo
(GWEE-rah)
page 13

23

Note to Parents and Teachers

Reading for information is an important part of a child's literacy development. Learning begins with a question about something. Help children think of themselves as investigators and researchers by encouraging their questions about the world around them. Each chapter in this book begins with a question that helps categorize the types of things that build. Read each question together. Look at the pictures. Can children think of other building things in each category? Discuss where you might find the answers. Assist children in using the picture glossary and the index to practice new vocabulary and research skills.

Index

Answers to quiz on page 22

Spiders, people, orioles, and beavers can build.

Robots can build, but not by themselves.